How to Draw the Life and Times of
Calvin Coolidge

Heidi Leigh Johansen

The Rosen Publishing Group's
PowerKids Press™
New York

Published in 2006 by The Rosen Publishing Group, Inc.
29 East 21st Street, New York, NY 10010

First Edition

Editor: Daryl Heller
Layout Design: Albert Hanner, Greg Tucker
Photo Researcher: Cindy Reiman

Illustrations: All illustrations by Albert Hanner.
Photo Credits: Pp. 4, 12 Amherst College Archives and Special Collections; pp. 7, 24, 26 ©
Bettmann/Corbis; p. 8 © Lee Snider/Photo Images/Corbis; p. 9 © Raymond Gehman/Corbis; p. 10
Vermont Division for Historic Preservation, President Calvin Coolidge State Historic Site, photograph by
Sherman Howe; p. 14 © Lake County Museum/Corbis; pp. 16, 20, 28 © Getty Images; p. 18 (top)
American Textile History Museum, Lowell, Massachusetts; p. 18 (bottom) Library of Congress Prints and
Photographs Division; p. 22 © AP/ Wide World Photos.

Library of Congress Cataloging-in-Publication Data

Johansen, Heidi Leigh.
    How to draw the life and times of Calvin Coolidge / Heidi Leigh Johansen.
        p. cm. — (A kid's guide to drawing the presidents of the United States of America)
    Includes index.
    ISBN 1-4042-3006-8 (library binding)
    1. Coolidge, Calvin, 1872–1933—Juvenile literature. 2. Presidents—United States—Biography—
Juvenile literature. 3. Drawing—Technique—Juvenile literature. I. Title. II. Series.
    E792.J64 2006
    973.91'5'092—dc22
                                            2005009069

Printed in China

Contents

A Quiet New Englander

John Calvin Coolidge was a quiet and hardworking man. He came from a small Vermont town and spent most of his life as a politician. In 1923, at the age of 51, Coolidge became the thirtieth president of the United States.

Coolidge was born to John and Victoria Moor Coolidge on July 4, 1872, in Plymouth Notch, Vermont. His father was a justice of the peace, a farmer, and a general storekeeper. Victoria Moor Coolidge, who died when Calvin was only 12 years old, encouraged her son's love of literature.

Young Coolidge attended school in a one-room stone building in Plymouth Notch. Around 1886, at the age of 14, Coolidge began high school at the Black River Academy in nearby Ludlow. Coolidge spent four years at the academy. He then spent a few months studying to prepare for college. His study paid off, and Coolidge was accepted to Amherst College in Amherst, Massachusetts.

After graduating from Amherst in 1895, Coolidge took a job as a law clerk in Northampton, Massachusetts. During this time he studied law and made political connections by meeting and talking with people in the local Republican Party. Coolidge passed the Massachusetts bar examination to become a lawyer on June 29, 1897.

The following year Coolidge was elected as a city councilman in Northampton. In 1905, Calvin Coolidge married a young teacher named Grace Goodhue. Soon after, the young politician was elected mayor of Northampton.

You will need the following supplies to draw the life and times of Calvin Coolidge:

√ A sketch pad   √ An eraser   √ A pencil   √ A ruler

These are some of the shapes and drawing terms you need to know:

Horizontal Line	——	Squiggly Line	∿
Oval	⬭	Trapezoid	▱
Rectangle	▭	Triangle	△
Shading	▰	Vertical Line	|
Slanted Line	/	Wavy Line	∿

To the Presidency

Many people believe that "Silent Cal," as Calvin Coolidge came to be called, was lucky when it came to politics. Though he worked hard, Coolidge was fortunate because a number of opportunities came his way that advanced his career. He served as state senator, state senate president, lieutenant governor, and finally as governor of Massachusetts in 1919.

Coolidge was chosen as the Republican vice presidential candidate in 1920. He ran with Warren G. Harding, the presidential candidate. They won the election and took office on March 4, 1921. When President Harding died suddenly in 1923, Coolidge became president. This was a prosperous time for many Americans. Coolidge successfully ran for president against John W. Davis, a Democrat, in 1924. In Coolidge's second term, his government passed several bills, including tax cuts that mainly helped wealthy Americans. With more money in their paychecks and bank accounts, Americans invested, or put money, in the stock market in record numbers.

On January 17, 1929, President Coolidge signed the Kellogg-Briand Pact. This international, or global, agreement was created after eight million people were killed in World War I. Nations that signed this pact promised to end conflicts without going to war.

Coolidge's Vermont Home

Calvin Coolidge was born in this house in Plymouth Notch, Vermont.

Vermont

Map of the United States of America

Calvin Coolidge was born in Plymouth Notch, which is a small Vermont town in the hills of the Green Mountains. The town consisted of a store, a schoolhouse, a church, and several homes. Today visitors can go to the President Calvin Coolidge State Historic Site in Plymouth Notch, where many of the town's buildings have been preserved. Visitors will learn about President Coolidge's childhood and what life was like in an early twentieth-century country town.

Coolidge was born in the downstairs bedroom of a small home, which was connected to the Plymouth Notch general store. At the age of four, Coolidge moved with his family to a larger house across the road, where he spent the remaining years of his boyhood. This boyhood home is called the Coolidge Homestead. It was here that Coolidge was sworn in as U.S. president in 1923. On display at the homestead are the beds, blankets, shavers, pots and pans, and shoes that Calvin Coolidge once used. In the kitchen is a wood box that young Calvin kept filled with firewood.

In 1947, the state of Vermont began acquiring buildings and land in Plymouth Notch. This was done to preserve the childhood hometown of the nation's thirtieth president.

The building on the right contained the Plymouth Notch general store, which Calvin Coolidge's father owned. As an adult Calvin Coolidge returned to Plymouth Notch almost every summer to help out on his family's farm. Coolidge later wrote about Plymouth Notch, "It would be hard to imagine better surroundings for . . . a boy than those which I had." In Vermont Coolidge felt he could get close to nature.

A Vermont Childhood

Life in a small Vermont town meant a lot of hard work in the early twentieth century. Calvin Coolidge did many chores to help his family. His chores included caring for the family's animals, chopping wood for the fire, fixing fences, and tapping, or  getting sap from, maple trees in April. Buckets, such as the one shown above, which Coolidge used, were needed to collect sap. However, Coolidge did have time to play. He loved to ride horseback and go ice-skating in the winter months.

In early 1885, Coolidge's mother was hurt in an accident caused by a runaway horse. She died some days later. Calvin and his younger sister, Abigail, never forgot their mother. Calvin visited her gravesite in Plymouth Notch whenever he could. Not long after his mother's death, Coolidge was sent to Black River Academy in nearby Ludlow, Vermont. At the school he took classes in history, mathematics, Greek, Latin, and literature.

1

Maple buckets, such as the one on the opposite page, were connected to a maple tree that had been tapped. The tap was drilled into the tree. In the spring the maple sap would drip from the tap into the bucket. Begin by drawing a rectangle.

2

From the top to the bottom of the rectangle, draw two slightly slanted guides. Between the two guides, near the top, draw two ovals. Draw one oval inside a slightly larger oval. The larger oval should touch the guides. The smaller oval may overlap the larger oval on top.

3

Draw four more ovals as shown. Add two ovals near the middle and two ovals not far from the bottom. Notice how the bottom ovals on these two sets of ovals are slightly wider than the ovals that are drawn above it.

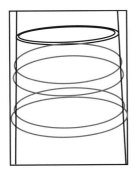

4

Add two more ovals. Then draw a curved line to create the bottom of the bucket.

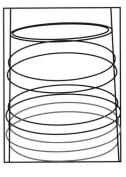

5

Erase the guides that extend above and below the bucket. Erase the ovals that are behind the bucket. Add six curved lines to the lines that remain. Add two shapes to the top. Add a small hook to the top left.

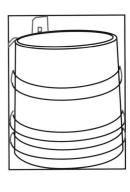

6

Erase the guide rectangle. Add vertical lines to create the strips of wood that make up the bucket. Two lines go inside the bucket at the top.

7

Erase the lines that are inside the horizontal rings. Finish by shading the bucket with the side of a pencil. The bucket is on display at the Coolidge Historic Site in Plymouth Notch.

Coolidge Attends Amherst College

Thanks to his many hours of study at the Black River Academy, Calvin Coolidge was accepted at Amherst College in Amherst, Massachusetts, in 1891. Coolidge was not an outstanding student in his first two years at Amherst. He did better in  his junior and senior years with the guidance of two teachers. These teachers were Charles E. Garman, a philosophy and religion teacher, and Anson D. Morse, a history teacher. Coolidge also became interested in public speaking, and this helped him be more outgoing and make more friends.

Coolidge became known at college for his odd, sly humor. In his senior year, he accepted an invitation to join the fraternity Phi Gamma Delta. Coolidge's classmates elected him to give a graduation speech at College Hall, which is shown above. By the time he graduated cum laude, or with honors, in 1895, Coolidge had decided that he wanted to "be of some use in the world." To accomplish that goal, Coolidge wanted to study to become a lawyer.

1

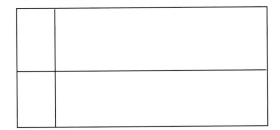

To begin drawing College Hall at Amherst College, draw a rectangle. Add a vertical guide and a horizontal guide as shown.

2

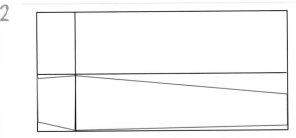

Draw two shapes in the bottom left and bottom right sections of the rectangle as shown. These shapes are created by drawing four slanted lines.

3

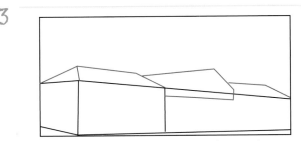

Erase the two guides. However, leave the part of the line that is the edge of the building on the left. Begin drawing the three sections of the roof as shown.

4

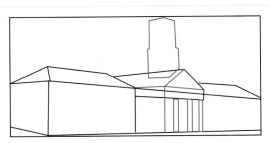

Begin the outline of the clock tower. Add lines to the roof of the center section. Draw three columns. Add a vertical line on the left to make the corner of the center section.

5

Add nine rectangular chimneys to the roof. Add the details to the clock tower as shown. These details are made using circles, slanted lines, and rectangles.

6

Erase extra lines. Draw the windows on the left portion of the building. However, be sure to leave a space in the center that will later be used to draw a tree.

7

Erase the rectangular guide and extra lines. Add windows to the right side of the building.

8

Add trees and a lawn to the front of the building. Use short and long lines. Shade the building, lawn, and leaves.

The Young Lawyer

After graduation in 1895, Calvin Coolidge became a clerk at the law firm of Hammond and Field in Northampton, Massachusetts. Becoming a law clerk

was a way for young people to learn about the law and study for the bar examination. During this time Coolidge read history and law books.

In June 1897, Coolidge passed the Massachusetts bar examination. The following February he opened his own law practice on Main Street in Northampton.

Coolidge was drawn into local politics after he attended meetings held by the Republican Party. In 1898, he was elected a city councilman. Two years later Coolidge served as Northampton's city lawyer. The courthouse where he worked is shown above. Coolidge also became Hampshire County's court clerk and chairman of the city's Republican Party.

1

Use a ruler to begin drawing the courthouse. Draw a rectangle. Add four diagonal guidelines as shown. Two are set close together.

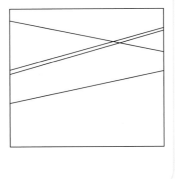

2

Draw three rectangles that sit along the base of the large rectangle. All three rectangles are positioned to the left of the three intersecting guidelines.

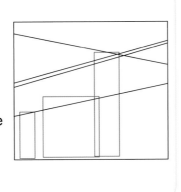

3

Erase extra lines as shown. Add two more rectangles along the base. Add the straight lines above those rectangles as shown.

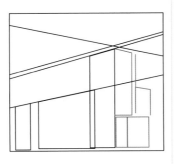

4

Erase extra lines. Add rooftops. Add three decorative shapes to the highest roof. Add the shape above the rectangles you drew in step 3. Add a small line to connect the shapes on the far left.

5

Erase extra lines. Add horizontal and slanted lines across the building. Add vertical lines to the top of the tallest section. Draw three windows that jut out of the roof. Add the chimney on the left.

6

Add windows to each floor of the building. Some windows have curved tops, others have straight lines. Draw the two staircases on the left and right sides.

7

Erase extra lines. Draw the decorative trim around some of the windows that have curved tops. Add horizontal lines to the building.

8

Finish with shading. Notice which areas are darker. The courthouse in Northampton was built between 1885 and 1887.

The Coolidge Family

During his first years in Northampton, Calvin Coolidge lived at a boardinghouse. One morning Coolidge was shaving while wearing a hat. A woman named  Grace Goodhue saw him through the window and laughed. Coolidge soon asked the owner of the boardinghouse to introduce him to her. Goodhue was a teacher at the Clarke Institute for the Deaf. The two began enjoying outings, walks, and streetcar rides together. Coolidge was 33 years old and Goodhue was 26 when the couple married on October 4, 1905. The Coolidges lived at 21 Massasoit Street in Northampton. Their first son, John, was born in 1906. Another son, Calvin Jr., arrived in 1908.

Calvin Coolidge and his wife had such different personalities that many people thought they were an odd couple. Grace was outgoing, while her husband was shy and quiet. Despite these differences the two were married for more than 27 years.

1

To begin drawing Grace Goodhue Coolidge draw a circle. To the left of the circle, draw an oval that is tilted slightly to the right.

2

Use a ruler to draw a vertical guide for the body as shown. Add a slanted horizontal guide for the shoulders. Add a circle at one end of the horizontal guide and an oval at the other.

3

Draw the outline of the side of her face along the left of the oval. Add an eyebrow and a guide for her eye. Add a small, tilted oval for her ear. Add four slanted lines to help you place her elbows and wrists.

4

Continue drawing her body. Draw shoulders, a neck, and arms using the circles and short diagonal lines as guides. Add a curved neckline to her dress. Note how the body lines curve.

5

Erase the body and shoulder guidelines. Using the guides draw the outline for the hair, eyes, and ear. Add lines to make the bottom of her dress. Draw the front of her dress using curved and wavy lines.

6

Erase extra lines. Add a dark pupil to her eye and a line to her nose. Draw her hands. Notice how the fingers are positioned on each hand. Draw some creases and folds on her dress.

7

Shade in her dress with light bands of color. The background and her hair are darker than her dress.

Massachusetts Politics

Calvin Coolidge was elected to the Massachusetts house of representatives in 1906 and again in 1907. There he voted for the Women's Suffrage Amendment, a six-day workweek, and shorter workdays for women and children. In 1909, Coolidge was elected mayor of Northampton. During his two terms, Coolidge helped lower the town's debt and improve the city's streets and sidewalks. He also hired additional police officers and firefighters and increased schoolteachers' pay.

Coolidge was elected to the Massachusetts state senate in 1911. In early 1912, thousands of textile, or cloth, workers went on strike in Lawrence, Massachusetts. The strikers are shown above. Coolidge was the chairman of a committee formed to settle the strike. To end the strike, he arranged for an increase in the workers' pay. Two years later Coolidge became president of the Massachusetts senate.

1

The girls in the top picture on the opposite page are winding thread onto a bobbin. Bobbins are used in textile, or cloth-making, mills. After thread is wound onto a bobbin, the bobbin is placed inside a machine. Draw a rectangle to begin creating a bobbin.

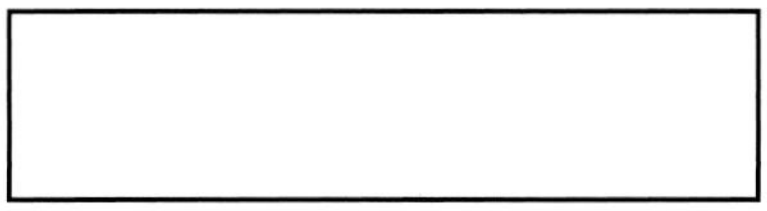

2

Draw the outline of the bobbin. The bobbin is drawn diagonally across the length of the rectangular guide. The bobbin slants down from the top left corner to the bottom right.

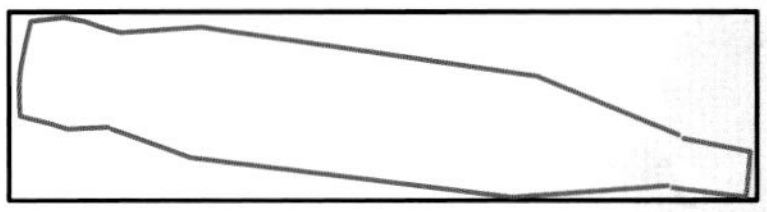

3

Add lines to the ends of the bobbin as shown. You will add four lines to the left side and one line to the right side.

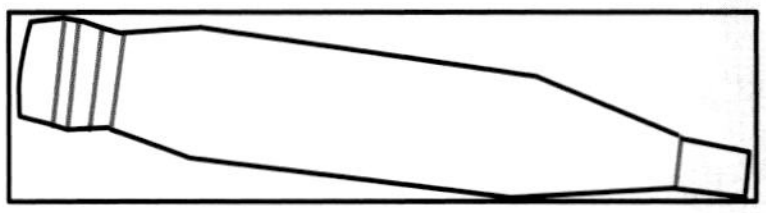

4

Add lines to the center portion of the bobbin. Make your lines evenly spaced. This will be the thread that is wound around the bobbin.

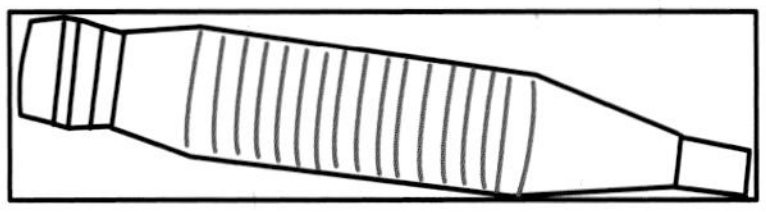

5

Use your pencil to lightly shade in the bobbin. The ends of the bobbin are much darker than the center of the bobbin.

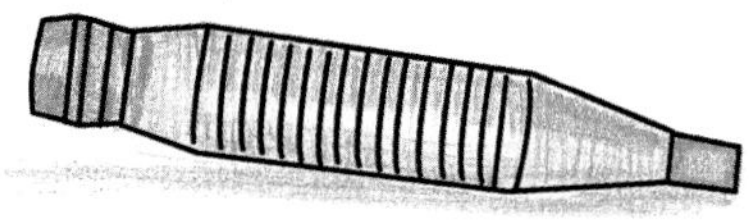

Lieutenant Governor and Governor

Calvin Coolidge successfully ran for lieutenant governor of Massachusetts in 1915. He was reelected twice and served as lieutenant governor until 1918. In this post he assisted Governor Samuel McCall. Coolidge was made chairman

of the state finance and pardoning committees. During this time the United States fought in World War I.

In 1919, 46-year-old Coolidge became governor of Massachusetts. That year the Boston police went on strike to protest low wages. After one day of violence and theft, Boston mayor Andrew Peters called in state troops. On the third day of the strike, Governor Coolidge sent additional state troops to Boston. He is shown above looking over the state troops. Coolidge supported police commissioner Edwin Curtis, when he fired 19 leaders of the strike. Of the Boston police strike, Governor Coolidge said, "There is no right to strike against the public safety by anybody, anywhere, any time." The strike ended soon after.

1

The local armed forces were called in to keep order during the Boston police strike. To begin drawing the soldier, draw a circle and an oval guide as shown.

2

Add a vertical line beneath the circle and the oval. Draw a slightly slanted line as shown. Add a circle for the left shoulder. Make a small diagonal line below the circle as a guide to position the elbow.

3

Draw the basic outline of the soldier's coat. The coat collar has two pieces. Draw the sleeve on the left. Add the bottom of his coat. The coat is made from straight and curving lines.

4

Erase extra lines. Add part of his other arm by the gun. Draw an oval for his ear and add three lines as guides for his face. Use curved lines to draw his legs and feet.

5

Erase the head guide and the diagonal guide. Draw his hair, eye, and nose. Add lines for his mouth, chin, and ear. Add a strap to the hat along the side of his face. Draw three buttons on the coat. Add lines to the coat and sleeve. Draw both hands around the gun.

6

Erase the face guides and the lines that go through the hands. Add lines to the soldier's hat, including two rounded shapes. Draw the details on his shoes.

7

Use the side of your pencil to shade in the drawing. Soldiers were needed during the Boston police strike because almost 80 percent of the Boston police force refused to go to work. Although many of the striking policemen lost their jobs, the new policemen got additional benefits.

A Vice President Takes Over

Many people praised Calvin Coolidge for his leadership during the police strike. Some thought he might even win the 1920 Republican presidential nomination.

However, Warren G. Harding received the Republican presidential nomination in June. Coolidge was nominated for vice president. Harding and Coolidge won by a large margin against Democratic nominees James M. Cox and Franklin D. Roosevelt. As vice president, Coolidge led the U.S. Senate, made speeches, and attended meetings.

In the summer of 1923, President Harding died suddenly in San Francisco, California. The news reached Coolidge early in the morning in Vermont. Messengers knocked on the door of his father's house, where Coolidge was visiting. Early the next morning on August 3, 1923, Coolidge's father, a notary public, gave his son the oath of office in front of a group of witnesses by the light of a kerosene lamp.

1 Calvin Coolidge was sworn in as president several hours before dawn. A kerosene lamp was needed so Coolidge, his father, and the other officials could see what they were doing. To begin drawing the kerosene lamp from the image on page 22, draw a rectangle.

2 Draw three ovals and a diagonal line as shown. These will be the guides. The top oval is smaller than the other ovals. The line on the bottom will create the base of the lamp.

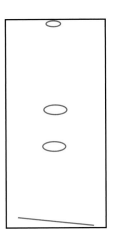

3 Draw a circle above the middle oval as shown. Next draw a large oval around the bottom two smaller ovals. This is tricky, so look at the drawing before you begin. Add a base to the lamp as shown using curving lines.

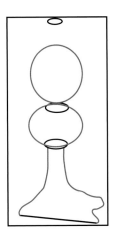

4 Connect the oval on the top to the large circle with two curving lines. Then connect the large circle to the oval below it with two short curving lines. The lines should hit the sides of the small oval as shown. Erase the top lines of the large oval and two smaller ovals.

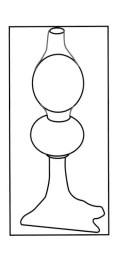

5 Add three small ovals across the middle section of the lamp. Draw wavy lines as shown near the base of the lamp. Add some wavy shapes near the top of the lamp as shown. These wavy shapes will be flames.

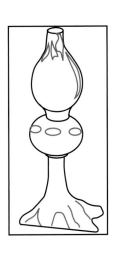

6 Use the side of your pencil to shade in the kerosene lamp. The top part of the lamp is lighter than the middle and the base of the lamp. Kerosene is a type of oil that is flammable, or something that catches fire easily.

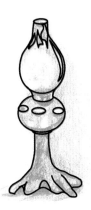

The Teapot Dome Scandal

Although Americans were in mourning for President Harding in August 1923, President Coolidge and the nation soon faced a scandal concerning members of Harding's cabinet. Teapot Dome was an oil-rich area in Wyoming that belonged to the U.S.

government. Several cabinet members had allowed private companies to drill for oil on this land. This illegal activity was carried out by Albert B. Fall, who had accepted more than $400,000 in bribes, and by Edwin Denby and Harry M. Daugherty.

President Coolidge publicly stated that he would punish the men who had committed the crimes. Albert B. Fall was sentenced to one year in prison. Denby and Daugherty both resigned, or gave up, their positions. President Coolidge's actions during the Teapot Dome scandal brought him respect from the American public. Teapot Rock, for which the Teapot Dome area was named, is shown above.

1

Wyoming's Teapot Rock got its name because part of the rock looks like the curved spout, or opening, of a teapot. To begin draw a rectangle.

2

Using a ruler add five guidelines, which will help you create Teapot Rock. Two of the lines are horizontal, one is vertical, and the other two are diagonal.

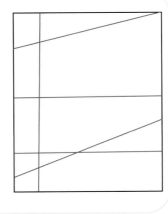

3

Draw the outline of the rock using curving lines. Before you begin notice where the outline touches the guides.

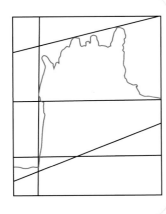

4

Erase the diagonal guides. Add more lines to the rock as shown. The line in the middle is a crack in the rock. The line at the bottom is where the rock comes out from the ground.

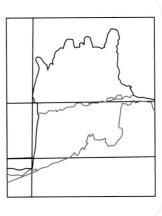

5

Erase the rest of the guidelines. Use squiggly lines to add crevices, or cracks, to the top portion of the rock. By drawing these crevices, you will make your drawing of the rock look more lifelike.

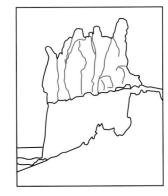

6

Use more squiggly lines to add crevices to the bottom half of the rock.

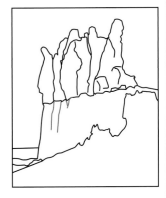

7

Use the side of a pencil to shade in the rock. Make the crevices of the rock darker than the rest of the rock's surface. The ground is lighter in color than the rock.

Keep Cool with Coolidge

Calvin Coolidge's ability to take charge after President Harding's death earned him the 1924 presidential nomination. Republican banners urged voters to "Keep Cool with Coolidge!" During this time the Coolidges suffered a tragedy in July 1924 when Calvin Jr. died.

Coolidge and Vice President Charles G. Dawes were elected on November 4, 1924. Coolidge was a conservative politician. He did not believe in making new laws that would increase the federal government's role in national affairs. During his presidency many tax cuts were approved and the national debt was reduced by more than $5 billion. Many federal taxes were lowered for wealthy citizens, who were encouraged to invest money in the stock market. The government did not impose many controls over large companies. Farmers, however, were struggling. Coolidge had opposed Congress's McNary-Haugen Farm Bill, which proposed government purchase of farmers' surplus, or crops that had not been sold.

1

An elephant is often used as a symbol of the Republican Party. To begin drawing one of the buttons from Coolidge's Republican presidential campaign, draw a circle.

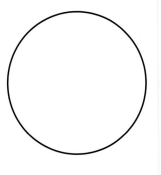

2

Inside this circle draw one small circle and one large oval. The circle is for the elephant's head. The oval is for the elephant's body.

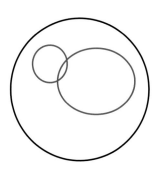

3

Draw the elephant's body, legs, and tail around the oval guide. Use the circle guide to draw the outline of the elephant's head and trunk. Add a small oval guide for the elephant's ear.

4

Draw the eye, mouth, and tusk. Use a squiggly line to create the shape of the ear. Draw the blanket on the elephant's back. It has two horizontal lines across it.

5

Erase the ear oval and the extra line in the tusk. Write the word "COOLIDGE" on the top section of the blanket on the elephant's back.

6

Write the word "AND" in the middle section of the blanket. Write the word "DAWES" in the bottom portion.

7

Use the side of your pencil to shade in the Republican campaign button. Make the background and parts of the blanket darker than the elephant.

Last Years

Calvin Coolidge was ready to retire after his second term. His son's death had affected him greatly. Coolidge did not run for president again in 1928. He left the White House in March 1929.

During his presidency many big businesses had thrived. Coolidge's tax cuts had encouraged wealthy Americans to invest heavily in the stock market. This proved to be a risky practice. The stock market could not keep going up. The value of the stocks came tumbling down in October 1929. The crash and the rush to remove money from the stock market and banks gave way to the Great Depression. This period was a time of hardship for many Americans during the 1930s.

Coolidge's final years were spent on his estate in Northampton, Massachusetts. He spent his time writing his autobiography, or life history, and articles. Calvin Coolidge died of a heart attack on January 5, 1933. The nation mourned a man who had risen from a tiny Vermont town all the way to the White House.

1

To begin drawing President Calvin Coolidge, use a ruler to draw a rectangle.

2

Draw an oval guide for the head and a smaller oval on the left side for the ear. Draw a vertical line from the bottom of the larger oval.

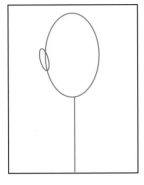

3

Add a few short, slightly slanted lines for the eyes, nose, and mouth. Draw a longer horizontal line for the shoulders. This line is also slightly slanted.

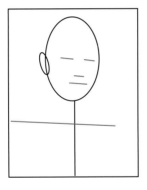

4

Draw the outline of the body using curved lines. Add the eyebrows, eyes, and nose.

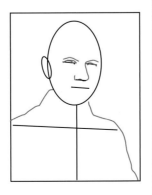

5

Erase the body, eyes, and nose guides. Draw the outline of the hair and chin. Add pupils to the eyes and draw a mouth. Erase the part of the small ear oval that intersects with the head. Add details to the ear. Draw the jacket collar and vest as shown.

6

Erase any remaining guides. Add the hairline on Coolidge's forehead. Add lines around his mouth and chin as shown. Draw the shirt collar and necktie.

7

Use the side of your pencil to shade in the jacket, the tie, and his hair. Shade his face and shirt, too. The background goes from dark to light. Notice how the shading is lightest near Coolidge's head.

Timeline

1872 John Calvin Coolidge is born in Plymouth Notch, Vermont, on July 4.

1895 Coolidge graduates from Amherst College.

1897 Coolidge passes the Massachusetts bar examination and is officially allowed to practice law in Massachusetts.

1898 Coolidge is elected a Northampton city councilman.

1905 Calvin Coolidge and Grace Goodhue are married.

1906 Coolidge is elected to the Massachusetts house of representatives. He serves for two terms.

1909 Coolidge is elected mayor of Northampton. He is reelected mayor for a second term.

1911 Coolidge is elected to the Massachusetts state senate. He becomes president of the senate in 1914.

1915 Coolidge is elected lieutenant governor of Massachusetts.

1919 Coolidge becomes governor of Massachusetts. He orders additional state troops to Boston after the Boston police force goes on strike.

1920 Coolidge is elected vice president of the United States.

1923 President Warren G. Harding dies suddenly, and Coolidge becomes the thirtieth president of the United States.

1924 Coolidge is elected president.

1929 Coolidge retires. He and his wife return to the family estate in Northampton, Massachusetts.

1933 John Calvin Coolidge dies in Northampton, Massachusetts, on January 5, 1933.

Glossary

amendment (uh-MEND-ment) An addition or a change to the Constitution.

bar examination (BAR ig-za-muh-NAY-shun) A state test taken by people who want to practice law.

boardinghouse (BOR-ding-hows) A house for lodging where meals are served.

bribes (BRYBZ) Money or favors given in return for something else.

cabinet (KAB-nit) A group of people who act as advisers to important government officials.

committees (kuh-MIH-teez) Groups of people directed to oversee or consider a matter.

conservative (kun-SER-vuh-tiv) Favoring a policy of keeping things as they are.

councilman (KOWN-sul-mun) A government official who helps run a city or town.

fraternity (fruh-TER-nuh-tee) A group of men who share a common interest.

justice of the peace (JUHS-tis UV THUH PEES) A judge who acts on lower court cases and who can perform marriages and other official tasks.

lawyer (LOY-er) One who gives advice about the law and speaks for people in court.

literature (LIH-tuh-ruh-chur) Writings such as books, plays, and poetry.

margin (MAR-jun) A measured amount.

nomination (nah-muh-NAY-shun) The suggestion that someone or something should be given an award or a position.

notary public (NOH-teh-ree PUH-blik) A person who checks law papers and records to make sure that they are real before putting an official seal on them.

oath (OHTH) A promise.

philosophy (feh-LAH-suh-fee) The study of human beliefs.

prosperous (PROS-prus) Successful and wealthy.

scandal (SKAN-dul) Behavior that people find shocking and bad.

site (SYT) The place where a certain event happens or happened.

suffrage (SUH-frij) The right of voting.

thrived (THRYVD) Fared or did well.

tragedy (TRA-jeh-dee) A very sad event.

violence (VY-lens) Strong force used to cause harm.

World War I (WURLD WOR WUN) The war fought between the Allies and the Central Powers from 1914 to 1918.

Index

Web Sites

Due to the changing nature of Internet links, PowerKids Press has developed an online list of Web sites related to the subject of this book. This site is updated regularly. Please use this link to access the list:
www.powerkidslinks.com/kgdpusa/coolidge/